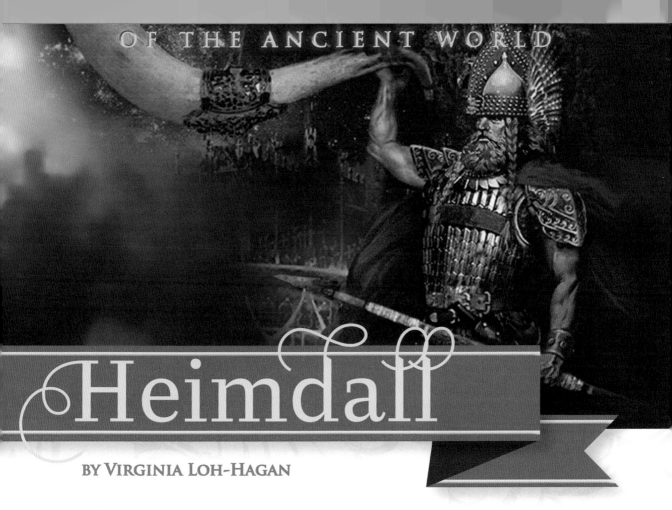

OF THE ANCIENT WORLD

Heimdall

BY VIRGINIA LOH-HAGAN

Gods and goddesses were the main characters of myths. Myths are traditional
stories from ancient cultures. Storytellers answered questions about the world by
creating exciting explanations. People thought myths were true. Myths explained
the unexplainable. They helped people make sense of human behavior and nature.
Today, we use science to explain the world. But people still love myths. Myths may
not be literally true. But they have meaning. They tell us something about our
history and culture.

45th Parallel Press

Published in the United States of America by Cherry Lake Publishing
Ann Arbor, Michigan
www.cherrylakepublishing.com

Content Adviser: Alexandra Krasowski, Worcester Art Museum, Harvard University (Extension School)
Reading Adviser: Marla Conn MS, Ed., Literacy specialist, Read-Ability, Inc.
Book Design: Jen Wahi

Photo Credits: © FABRIZIO CONTE/Shutterstock.com, 5; WG Collingwood/Public Domain/Wikimedia Commons, 6; Carl Emil Doepler/Public Domain/Wikimedia Commons, 8; © Marzolino/Shutterstock.com, 11; © Vadim Sadovski/Shutterstock.com, 13; Nils Blommer/Public Domain/Wikimedia Commons, 15; © Fotokostic/Shutterstock.com, 17; Icelandic Manuscript, SAM 66/Public Domain/Wikimedia Commons, 19; © Ilkin Zeferli/Shutterstock.com, 22; © Fotokvadrat/Shutterstock.com, 25; © Luba V Nel/Shutterstock.com, 27; © Dreamer Company/Shutterstock.com, 29; © Howard David Johnson, 2018, Cover, 1, 21; Various art elements throughout, Shutterstock.com

45th Parallel Press is an imprint of Cherry Lake Publishing.

Library of Congress Cataloging-in-Publication Data

Names: Loh-Hagan, Virginia, author.
Title: Heimdall / by Virginia Loh-Hagan.
Description: Ann Arbor : Cherry Lake Publishing, 2018. | Series: Gods and goddesses of the ancient world | Includes bibliographical references and index.
Identifiers: LCCN 2018003338 | ISBN 9781534129481 (hardcover) | ISBN 9781534131187 (pdf) | ISBN 9781534132689 (pbk.) | ISBN 9781534134386 (hosted ebook)
Subjects: LCSH: Heimdall (Norse deity)—Juvenile literature.
Classification: LCC BL870.H4 L64 2018 | DDC 293/.2113—dc23
LC record available at https://lccn.loc.gov/2018003338

Printed in the United States of America
Corporate Graphics

ABOUT THE AUTHOR:

Dr. Virginia Loh-Hagan is an author, university professor, former classroom teacher, and curriculum designer. Her voice is like a Gjallarhorn. She's very loud. She lives in San Diego with her very tall husband and very naughty dogs. To learn more about her, visit www.virginialoh.com.

TABLE OF CONTENTS

CHAPTER 1

SON OF NINE MOTHERS

Who is Heimdall? Who are his family members? What does he look like?

Heimdall was a **Norse** god. Norse means coming from Norway. Heimdall was one of the main gods. He was the **guardian** of the gods. Guardians are protectors. Heimdall was a **watchman**. Watchmen are people who guard. He watched for danger. He protected the gods from giants. Giants were the gods' enemies.

Heimdall had a magical horn. He had a magical horse. His horse was named Gulltoppr. It had a golden **mane**. Mane is horse hair. Heimdall had a sword. It was called Head. Heimdall was connected to rams.

He was called the white god. He had really white skin. He shone. He had golden teeth. He was tall. He was handsome.

He was born at the beginning of time. He was also one of the last gods to die. He came from a very **ancient** family line.

Heimdall was also a god of light.

Some believe Heimdall's mothers were nine giantesses and not the Nine Waves.

Ancient means old. His great-grandfather was an ancient giant king. His name was Fornjot. Fornjot's children were Aegir and Ran. Aegir and Ran were rulers of the sea. They were Heimdall's grandparents.

Odin was Heimdall's father. Odin was the father of all the gods. He went to sea. He saw nine sea goddesses. He fell in love. Together, they gave birth to Heimdall. Heimdall's mothers were the daughters of Aegir and Ran. They were wave **maidens**. Maidens are young women.

Family Tree

Grandparents: Borr (god of mountains), Bestla (giantess, goddess of water and ice), Aegir (god of the sea), and Ran (goddess of the sea)

Parents: Odin (father of all gods) and Nine Waves

Half brothers: Hod (god of winter and darkness, often called Hodr), Hermod (messenger of the gods), and Thor (god of thunder)

Children: Thrall (ancestor of servants), Karl (ancestor of craftsmen and farmers), and Jarl (ancestor of nobles and warriors)

His mothers were known as the Nine Waves. They were beautiful. They had the powers of the ocean. Dufa was a hidden wave. Kolga was a cold wave. Blodughadda was red sea foam. Bara was the moment a wave hit shore. Bylgja was a wave breaker. Hronn was a growing wave. Hefring was a rising wave. Unn was a foamy wave. Himinglava was a clear wave.

All nine mothers took care of Heimdall. They fed him the earth's strength. They fed him seawater. They fed him the sun's heat. Heimdall grew tall. He grew strong. He left his mothers. He went to Odin.

Heimdall's family controlled the world.

CHAPTER 2

GUARDIAN GOD

What is Heimdall's job? What are his special skills?

There were two tribes of Norse gods and goddesses. They were the Aesir and the Vanir. The Aesir gods lived in **Asgard**. Asgard was the center of the universe. It was the heavens. It was the highest of nine worlds. The worlds were connected by the World Tree.

Heimdall's job was to guard Bifrost. Bifrost was a rainbow bridge. It spanned Asgard and **Midgard**. Midgard was where humans lived. Bifrost was the only way into Asgard. The gods were worried of attacks from giants.

Heimdall lived at the top of Bifrost. His house was called Himinbjorg. This means "sky cliffs."

Heimdall sat at the bridge. He could see all the worlds. But he didn't meddle. He was on the border of the **divine** and human. Divine means godly. Heimdall could move between worlds. He kept watch all the time.

Heimdall had super hearing powers. He could hear grass grow. He could hear wool grow on a sheep's back. He had

Heimdall lived at the edge of the world.

All in the Family

Aegir and Ran ruled the sea. They were husband and wife. They lived in a grand hall. Halls are grand houses. They lived under the sea. They controlled the sea. Aegir means "ocean." He had white hair. He had a long beard. He had magical powers. He was a good host. He had fancy parties for the gods. He made his own beer. He had a spear. He made the seas calm. Ran means "robber." She caused sea storms. She was beautiful. She lured sailors. Then she drowned them. She dragged them to her home. She also had a net. She collected the victims of shipwrecks and storms. Aegir and Ran had nine daughters. The daughters were spirits of the wave. They gave birth to Heimdall. Vikings would throw prisoners into the sea. Vikings were Norse warriors. They wanted to keep Aegir and Ran happy.

Heimdall had the power to send beings to different worlds.

super eyesight. He could see at night. He could see things far in the distance. He didn't need to sleep. He was always awake. He was always alert. He could see the future. He could change forms.

CHAPTER 3

HELPER OF THE GODS

How does Heimdall help Freya? How does he help Thor?

Heimdall left Bifrost a few times. He did this to help the gods.

Freya was the goddess of beauty and war. She had the most beautiful necklace. It was named Brisingamen. This means "jewelry of fire." Loki was a trickster god. He stole her necklace. He ran away to the sea. He turned into a seal.

Freya asked Heimdall for help. He changed into a seal, too. He fought Loki. He got the necklace. He gave it back to Freya. But Loki never forgave Heimdall. They became enemies.

Heimdall was smart. He helped Thor. Thor was the god of thunder. He was Heimdall's half brother. Thor had a magical hammer. His hammer would return to him. It killed anything in its path. It was the most powerful weapon.

A giant stole Thor's hammer. He wanted to use it to marry Freya. Heimdall gave Thor an idea. He told Thor to dress

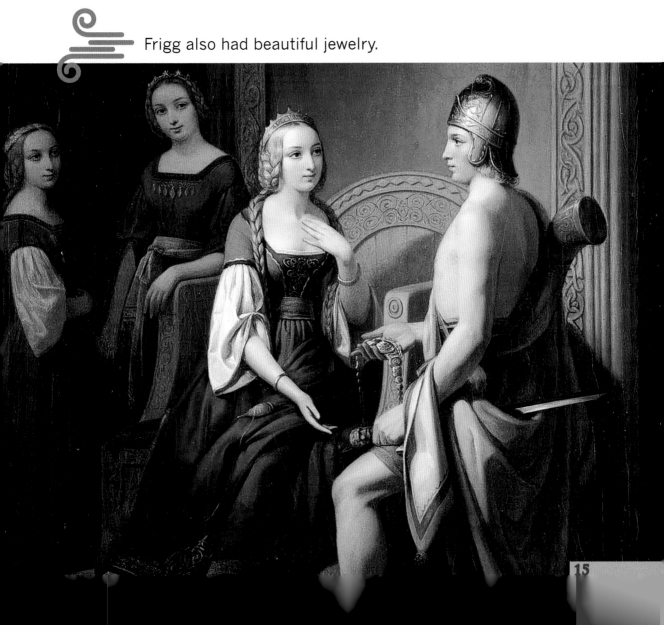

Frigg also had beautiful jewelry.

Real World Connection

The Minnesota Vikings is a football team. It's part of the National Football League. The team has a new stadium. The stadium opened in 2016. It has a Viking ship shaped like a dragon. It has a giant Gjallarhorn. It weighs 800 pounds (363 kilograms). It's hung from the ceiling. It's used before each home game. A special person is asked to blow the horn. Over 100 former Vikings players and coaches have blown the horn. Famous people have also blown the horn. The horn signals the coming of the team players. The players rush onto the field. The horn is also blown when the Vikings score. The Gjallarhorn is a big sound system. It's in the shape of Heimdall's horn. The Vikings had a giant Gjallarhorn at their old stadium. But it broke. The weather was too cold. The horn snapped in half during an important game. The Vikings lost.

Thor's hammer was named Mjollnir.

like a bride. Thor borrowed Freya's necklace. The giant used the hammer to **hallow** the wedding. Hallow means to bless. Thor grabbed the hammer. He crushed the giant. He got back his hammer.

CHAPTER 4

HORN BLOWER

What is Ragnarok? What does Heimdall do at Ragnarok? How does Heimdall die?

Loki caused the death of Baldur. Baldur was the god of light and sunshine. He was one of Odin's sons. His death led to winter. The winter lasted 3 years. Snow fell from all directions. The world became dark. This started **Ragnarok**. Ragnarok was the final battle. It was the end of the world. It was known as the "doom of the gods." The gods were worried. The balance of the world was upset. The gods were fated to die.

Heimdall trained for Ragnarok. He had his special horn.
His horn was called Gjallarhorn. This means "yelling horn."
It was really loud. It could be heard across all the worlds.

Heimdall's job was to watch for giants. He stood out in
the cold. He stood in the dark. He saw giants coming.

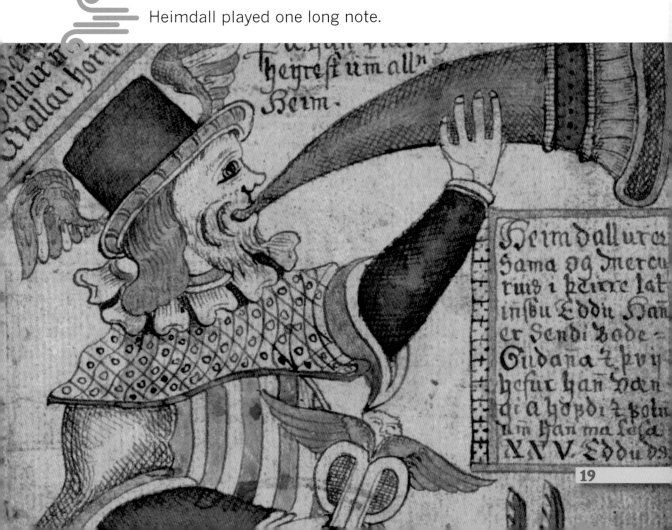

Heimdall played one long note.

He blew on Gjallarhorn. This warned the gods. The gods prepared for war.

Heimdall's horn meant giants had crossed Bifrost. Giants attacked Asgard. They wanted to kill the gods. Heimdall's horn brought everyone together. Gods came. Giants came. Other magical creatures came. They all met for the final battle. They met at Vigrid. Vigrid was a large battlefield.

Heimdall also saw Loki coming. Loki led an army of giants. He fought against the gods. His children were monsters. They helped him.

Hel was one of his children. Hel was a goddess of death. She gave her father an army of dead soldiers. Jormungand was Hel's brother. He was a big snake. He caused the seas to flood. His poison killed Thor.

 Heimdall wore white and silver armor.

Heimdall was a good swordsman.

Fenrir was also Hel's brother. He was a big wolf. He ran around the world. His lower jaw was on the ground. His upper jaw was in the sky. He ate everything in his way. He ate the sun. He killed Odin.

Heimdall fought Loki. They were the last ones to fight. They killed each other. Loki's army set the world on fire. This happened while they fought. The earth sank into the sea. Then, it rose again. The world started over.

Cross-Cultural Connection

Gabriel was an archangel. Archangels go between humans and God. Gabriel means "God is my strength." Muslims, Jews, and Christians believe in Gabriel. He's the angel of truth. He's the angel of revelation. He reveals things. He shares important messages. He interprets dreams. He shared the birth of Isaac, John the Baptist, and Jesus Christ. He protects people. People ask for Gabriel's help. He clears away confusion. He gives people wisdom. He gives people confidence. He guides people. Like Heimdall, he's connected to the color white. A beautiful white light shines on him. It makes things pure. Gabriel also blows a horn. He always has a big copper trumpet with him. He signals the Lord's return to earth. He also signals the coming of doom. A line in a famous song is "Blow, Gabriel, blow."

CHAPTER 5

FATHER OF MANKIND

Who is Rig? What are the three classes Heimdall created?

In some stories, Heimdall was known as Rig. Rig means "king." He was the father of mankind. He created the different **social classes**. Social classes are different groups in a society. He did this before guarding Bifrost.

Heimdall wandered around the world. He walked by the sea. He saw a farm. Ai and Edda worked on the farm. They gave him basic food. Heimdall left in the morning. Nine months later, Edda gave birth to a son. The son had dark hair. He was named Thrall. Thrall was strong.

He married Thir. They had 12 sons. They had nine daughters. They were good workers. They became the **ancestors** of servants. Ancestors are generations that came before the current one.

These social classes appeared in Norse society.

Heimdall kept walking. He saw a nice house. The house belonged to Afi and Amma. Afi and Amma were farmers and **craftsmen**. Craftsmen practice skills. Afi and Amma gave him good food. Heimdall left in the morning. Nine months later, Amma gave birth to a son. The son was named Karl. He had red hair. He married Snor. They had 12 sons. They had 10 daughters. They became the ancestors of farmers and craftsmen.

Heimdall kept walking. He saw a palace. The palace belonged to Faoir and Mooir. Faoir and Mooir were rulers. They gave him fancy food. Heimdall left in the morning. Nine months later, Mooir gave birth to a son. The son was named Jarl. He had blond hair. He was a good fighter. He was a good horse rider. He married Erna. He and Erna had 12 sons. They became the ancestors of warriors

Craftsmen make things. They fix things.

and nobles. Heimdall adopted Jarl. He gave Jarl his name.
He named him Rig.

Explained By Science

Sounds are waves. They're long waves. They're made from a
vibrating source. Vibrating is buzzing. A Gjallarhorn makes
sounds. It works like a trumpet. People blow trumpets. They
blow into a mouthpiece. They use their lip muscles. They blow
air. They do this quickly. They buzz into the mouthpiece. This
causes air to vibrate. This makes a sound wave in the trumpet.
The sound wave moves through the trumpet. It hits the end of
the trumpet. The sound wave changes direction. It reflects back
to the lips. The sound wave changes shape. Sound waves go
back and forth. This makes a standing wave. Energy is released
as sound. Sound is the buzzing of the lips being amplified. The
trumpet amplifies the sound. Amplifies means to make louder.

Nobles own land.

Don't anger the gods. Heimdall had great powers. And he knew how to use them.

DID YOU KNOW?

- Heimdall's name means "the one who illuminates the world." Illuminate means to bring to light. This means to let people know things.

- Heimdall was also known as Gullintanni. This means "the one with the golden teeth."

- Heimdall was also known as Vindler. This means "one protecting against the wind."

- Heimdall was featured in Marvel's *Thor* movies. He's played by Idris Elba. Instead of gold teeth, he has gold eyes.

- Heimdall's nine mothers may seem strange. But many cultures have stories about nine women. King Arthur stories have Morgan and her eight sisters. These women lived on the Island of Avalon. They saw the future. They healed. Welsh stories have nine maidens. They tended fires under a magical cauldron. Cauldrons are cooking pots. Greek stories have the nine muses. Muses inspire ideas.

- People can buy a ringtone for their cell phones that sounds like a Gjallarhorn.

- Odin was married to Frigg. Frigg was the goddess of marriage. But Odin had many lovers. He also had many sons. This means Heimdall had many half brothers. Frigg raised Heimdall. She was his stepmother.

- Heimdall grew up in water. Water was important to him. It's clear. He could see the heavens in the reflection.

- Some stories say Heimdall made a deal with the devil. He gave up one of his ears. He gained super hearing powers in his other ear.

CONSIDER THIS!

TAKE A POSITION! Heimdall's main job was to blow his horn. Do you think this was an important role? Why or why not? Argue your point with reasons and evidence.

SAY WHAT? Heimdall was a guardian god. He was a watchman. He was like the gods' bodyguard. Explain his role. Explain what he did.

THINK ABOUT IT! Heimdall blew a Gjallarhorn to warn others. Think of other sounds used to warn others. Make a list of the sounds and their purposes. Create your own warning sound. What would it sound like? What would its purpose be?

LEARN MORE

Napoli, Donna Jo, and Christina Balit (illust.). *Treasury of Norse Mythology: Stories of Intrigue, Trickery, Love, and Revenge.* Washington, DC: National Geographic, 2015.

Worley, Rob M., and Shawn Moll (illust.). *Heimdall.* Edina, MN: Magic Wagon, 2011.

GLOSSARY

ancestors (AN-ses-turz) previous generations from which current generations come from

ancient (AYN-shuhnt) old

Asgard (AHS-gahrd) center of the universe where the Aesir gods lived

craftsmen (KRAFTS-men) workers who practice skills like building tools and making clothes

divine (dih-VINE) godly

guardian (GAHR-dee-uhn) protector

hallow (HAL-oh) to bless or honor

maidens (MAY-duhnz) young women serving in the court of a royal person

mane (MAYN) the long hair on a horse

Midgard (MID-gahrd) middle of the universe where humans lived

Norse (NORS) coming from the Norway area

Ragnarok (RAHG-nuh-rok) the final battle of the gods' world, marking the end of their world

social classes (SOH-shuhl KLAS-ez) different groups of people in a society

watchman (WAHCH-muhn) someone who keeps watch or guards

INDEX